Meditation Cards

Elinor Von Linden

Schiffer
Publishing Ltd.

4880 Lower Valley Road Atglen, Pennsylvania 19310

Text by author unless otherwise noted
Images and image description courtesy of NASA, Hubblesite.org, The Hubble Heritage Team, and others as listed.
Back cover image: NGC 6397. Image Credit: NASA and The Hubble Heritage Team (AURA/STScI)
Acknowledgment: A. Cool (SFSU).

Cover design: Bruce Waters
Type set in UnivrstyRoman Bd BT/NewBskvll BT
ISBN: 978-0-7643-3899-1
Printed in China

Schiffer Books are available at special discounts for bulk purchases for sales promotions or premiums. Special editions, including personalized covers, corporate imprints, and excerpts can be created in large quantities for special needs. For more information contact the publisher:

Published by Schiffer Publishing Ltd.
4880 Lower Valley Road
Atglen, PA 19310
Phone: (610) 593-1777; Fax: (610) 593-2002
E-mail: Info@schifferbooks.com

For the largest selection of fine reference books on this and related subjects, please visit our

website at **www.schifferbooks.com**
We are always looking for people to write books on new and related subjects. If you have an idea for a book please contact us at the above address.

This book may be purchased from the publisher.
Include $5.00 for shipping.
Please try your bookstore first.

You may write for a free catalog.

In Europe, Schiffer books are distributed by
Bushwood Books
6 Marksbury Ave.
Kew Gardens
Surrey TW9 4JF England
Phone: 44 (0) 20 8392 8585; Fax: 44 (0) 20 8392 9876
E-mail: info@bushwoodbooks.co.uk
Website: www.bushwoodbooks.co.uk

Dedication

I would like to thank my daughter, Carrie, for the inspiration.

Acknowledgments

I would like to thank my friends in my astrology group for their support and my daughter, Lisa, for assisting in editing. I would also like to thank my spirit guide. I would not have been able to do this without them.

Sacred Space Meditation Cards

The God within connects with the Universal God.
We are all of the same vibration,
ever expanding, always creating.
The energy of the Universe
flows through everyone.
There is nothing you cannot be.
All Space is Sacred.

INTRODUCTION

The Great Cosmic Mind, which we are all a part of, created Planet Earth and the far reaches of the galaxies. The power, love, and goodness of the Creator, is within all of us. If we can draw on this energy and feel the force and potential, it can lead to peace and abundance.

We must go beyond the everyday traps the mind sets for us and go within.

We must sit and be quiet and listen. (Listen to the inner voices, as they keep the mind flowing towards a state of happiness and serenity.)

Spirit can be found in the smallest atom to the Universe and beyond.

Feel each galaxy and experience your personal power in each of the cards that follow.

~Elinor Von Linden

How To Use The Cards

While keeping an open mind, mentally ask your guides for help and direction. As you pick a card, focus on the question and feel immersed into the boundless and powerful universe. Here you can unite with the vast oneness. You can pick a card each day or as often as you want. With each card you can become deeply involved with the picture of the cosmos. Reading the book descriptions will help your vision and consciousness. Recite the affirmations as often as needed each day.

There are some specials points of interest directed by the Hubble contributors to this book describing locations within varied images. This then would reflect the orientation of those images. In the cases where such description is available, you will find an arrow on the text side of the card pointing you to the top of the image on the other side. Once you view the card from the perspective given in the description, feel free to meditate on the scene at any angle.

Focus

When I focus on goodness,
I can change my life—even the world.

AFFIRMATIONS

I Challenge behavior that no longer serves me and eliminate what is not useful in life.
I am clear about what I desire and focus on my highest priorities.
As I change my focus, I will change my life and beckon others.

The Image: Earth

This spectacular "blue marble" image is the most detailed true-color image of the entire Earth to date. Using a collection of satellite-based observations, scientists and visualizers stitched together months of observations of the land surface, oceans, sea ice, and clouds into a seamless, true-color mosaic of every square kilometer (.386 square mile) of our planet.

Photo and description courtesy of NASA

LEADERSHIP

I have great leadership qualities,
I am courageous and strong.
I know the Universal Spirit guides me along.

AFFIRMATIONS

As I take control of my own life, I know I have power and guidance.

My actions are divinely guided.

I am more powerful than I realize and I am tuned into many opportunities for achievement.

The Image: LMC-N49. Celestial Fireworks Galaxy N4

Resembling the puffs of smoke and sparks from a summer fireworks display, this Hubble image depicts the delicate filaments debris from a stellar explosion in a neighboring galaxy.

N-49, or DEM L 190, this remnant is from a massive star that died in a supernova blast whose light would have reached Earth thousands of years ago. This filamentary material will eventually be recycled into building new generations of stars. Our own sun and planets are constructed from similar debris of supernova that exploded in the Milky Way billions of years ago.

Photo and description courtesy of Hubblesite.org
Image Credit: NASA and The Hubble Heritage Team (STScI/AURA)
Acknowledgment: Y.-H. Chu (UIUC), S. Kulkarni (Caltech), and R. Rothschild (UCSD)

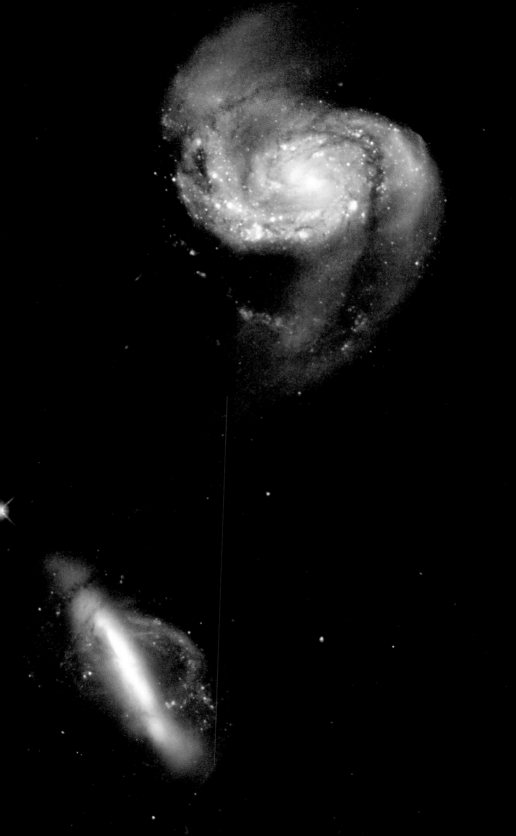

INTUITION

I follow my intuition, knowing the insight I receive
provides me with security and love.

AFFIRMATIONS

I Trust and follow my inner knowledge.

I recognize the loving guidance I hear within my heart, as it guides me in wonderful ways.

I am aware of my inner power and I intend to live with peace and love.

The Image: ARP-87

The pair, known collectively as Arp 87, is one of hundreds of interacting and merging galaxies known in our nearby universe. Two galaxies perform an intricate dance in this new Hubble Space Telescope image. The galaxies, containing a vast number of stars, swing past each other in a graceful performance choreographed by gravity.

Photo and description courtesy of Hubblesite.org
Image Credit: NASA, ESA, and the Hubble Heritage Team (STScI/AURA)

LISTEN

The Great Mind of God knows the answers
to my problems before I ever ask.

AFFIRMATIONS

As Source hears my thought and responds to my desires, I will listen to the small voice within me as it speaks the truth.
I will listen to someone today and respond with love.

The Image: NGC-1569

Astronomers have long puzzled over why a small, nearby, isolated galaxy is pumping out new stars faster than any galaxy in our local neighborhood. Now NASA's Hubble Space Telescope has helped astronomers solve the mystery of the loner starburst galaxy, called NGC-1569, by showing that it is one and a half times farther away than astronomers thought.

The farther distance not only means that the galaxy is intrinsically brighter, but also that it is producing stars two times faster than first thought. The galaxy is forming at a rate more than 100 times higher than in the Milky Way. This high star-formation rate has been almost continuous for the past 100 million years.

Photo and description courtesy of Hubblesite.org
Image Credit: NASA, ESA, the Hubble Heritage Team (STScI/AURA), and A. Aloisi (STScI/ESA)
Credit for Advanced Camera Data: NASA, ESA, A. Aloisi (STScI/ESA), J. Mack and A. Grocholski (STScI), M. Sirianni (STScI/ESA), R. van der Marel (STScI), L. Angeretti, D. Romano, and M. Tosi (INAF-OAB), and F. Annibali, L. Greggio, and E. Held (INAF-OAP)
Credit for Wide Field Planetary Camera 2 Data: NASA, ESA, P. Shopbell (California Institute of Technology), R. Dufour (Rice University), D. Walter (South Carolina State University, Orangeburg), and A. Wilson (University of Maryland, College Park)

LOVING WORDS

I lovingly hear the Universe bring the spirit of words to my mind,
and so I always speak with love.

AFFIRMATIONS

I am kind and gentle to myself and others.

I appreciate everyone I meet and speak in a gentle and loving voice.

I accept and respect others in the way I would like to be accepted.

My voice is always delicate and kind.

The Image: NGC 4013

NASA's Hubble Space Telescope has snapped this remarkable view of a perfectly "edge-on" galaxy, NGC 4013. This Hubble picture reveals with exquisite detail huge clouds of dust and gas extending along, as well as far above, the galaxy's main disk.

NGC 4013 is a spiral galaxy, similar to our own Milky Way, lying some 55 million light-years from Earth in the direction of the constellation Ursa Major. Viewed pole-on, it would look like a nearly circular pinwheel, but NGC 4013 happens to be seen edge-on from our vantage point. Even at 55 million light-years, the galaxy is larger than Hubble's field of view, and the image shows only a little more than half of the object, albeit with unprecedented detail.

Photo and description courtesy of Hubblesite.org
Image Credit: NASA and The Hubble Heritage Team (STScI/AURA)
Acknowledgment: J.C. Howk (Johns Hopkins University) and B.D. Savage (University of Wisconsin-Madison)

MANIFESTOR

I have the ability to use my creative
talents to achieve my desires.
All things are manifested in my own reality.

AFFIRMATIONS

My thoughts are the key to receiving my desires.
I stay in tune with my conscious self and know that the connection I have with the Universe is all I need to receive.
I am always open and ready to accept the riches of the Universe.

The Image: NGC 3603

Thousands of sparkling young stars are nestled within the giant nebula NGC 3603. This stellar "jewel box" is one of the most massive young star clusters in the Milky Way Galaxy.

NGC 3603 is a prominent star-forming region in the Carina spiral arm of the Milky Way, about 20,000 light-years away. This image from NASA's Hubble Space Telescope shows a young star cluster surrounded by a vast region of dust and gas. The image reveals stages in the life cycle of stars.

Photo and description courtesy of Hubblesite.org
Image Credit: NASA, ESA, and the Hubble Heritage (STScI/AURA)-ESA/Hubble Collaboration
Acknowledgment: J. Maíz Apellániz (Institute of Astrophysics of Andalucía, Spain)

ACTION

I know Source has given me
intuition and Divine guidance.
I act for my good and the good of others.

AFFIRMATIONS

I take charge of my life.
I do not worry about the future.
When I see an injustice, I will act on it if it is for everyone's highest good, and extend a hand to help others.
When action is required, I will respond with help from Source.
I know the Creator has provided me with all I need.
Today I will create a paradise in my life.

The Image: The Orion Nebula or M43

M43 or the Orion Nebula is a picture book of star formation, from the massive, young stars that are shaping the nebula to the pillars of dense gas that may be the homes of budding stars. The bright central region is the home of the four heftiest stars in the nebula. The stars are called the Trapezium because they are arranged in a trapezoid pattern. Ultraviolet light unleashed by these stars is carving a cavity in the nebula and disrupting the growth of hundreds of smaller stars. Located near the Trapezium stars are stars still young enough to have disks of material encircling them. These disks are called protoplanetary disks or "proplyds" and are too small to see clearly in this image. The disks are the building blocks of solar systems.

Photo and description courtesy of Hubblesite.org
Image Credit: NASA,ESA, M. Robberto (Space Telescope Science Institute/ESA) and the Hubble Space Telescope Orion Treasury Project Team

I AM WITHOUT LIMITS

The Universe is beyond the limits of our expansion, but not of God's Divine light.

AFFIRMATIONS

I see beyond what is visible and see all things in Divine Light.
My thoughts are powerful magnets and they reach out to the Universe.
As I access the power of the Universe, I then reflect the power of the Creator.

The Image: NGC 1132

The elliptical galaxy NGC 1132 reveals the final result of what may have been a group of galaxies that merged together in the recent past. Another possibility is that the galaxy formed in isolation as a "lone wolf" in a universe ablaze with galaxy groups and clusters. NGC 1132 is dubbed a "fossil group" because it contains enormous concentrations of dark matter, comparable to the dark matter found in an entire group of galaxies. NGC 1132 also has a strong X-ray glow from an abundant amount of hot gas that is normally only found in galaxy groups.

Photo and description courtesy of Hubblesite.org
Image Credit: NASA, ESA, and the Hubble Heritage (STScI/AURA)-ESA/Hubble Collaboration
Acknowledgment: M. West (ESO, Chile)

H A R M O N Y

My heart sings in harmony with the Universe.
I am always on key.

AFFIRMATIONS

I keep in tune with the vibrations of the Universe.

The rhythm of celestial voices is the source of energy that radiates from the Creator.

As long as I stay connected with this rhythm, I am in harmony and will continue to sing joyously.

The Image: NGC 1275

NGC 1275 is about 235 million light-years away in the constellation Perseus. Embedded in the center of a large cluster of galaxies known as the Perseus Cluster, it is also known to emit a powerful signal at both X-ray and radio frequencies. The galaxy collision causes the gas and dust already existing in the central bright galaxy to swirl into the center of the object. The X-ray and radio emission indicates the probable existence of a black hole at the bright galaxy's center.

Photo and description courtesy of Hubblesite.org
Image Credit: NASA and The Hubble Heritage Team (STScI/AURA)
Acknowledgment: M. Donahue (STScI) and J. Trauger (JPL)

LOVE

Love is the life current that flows through the Universe. This current fills my heart
as I surrender my will to God's will.

AFFIRMATIONS

I recognize my own value and live with self-love. Only then can I reflect back to others the
love I feel within.
Thoughts of love draw other thoughts of love.
I embrace the world with an open heart.
My passion is fueled by God's love.

The Image: NGC-3370

Amid a backdrop of far-off galaxies, the majestic dusty spiral, NGC 3370, looms
in the foreground in this NASA Hubble Space Telescope image. Observations
taken with the Advanced Camera for Surveys show intricate spiral arm structure
spotted with hot areas of new star formation. But this galaxy is more than just a
pretty face. Nearly 10 years earlier NGC 3370, in the constellation Leo, hosted a
bright exploding star. In November 1994, the light of a supernova in nearby NGC
3370 reached Earth. This stellar outburst briefly outshone all of the tens of billions
of other stars in its galaxy.

IMAGINE THE POSSIBILITIES

As I merge with my higher self, I am open to endless possibilities, and I am truly blessed.

AFFIRMATIONS

The everyday experiences of this world no longer serves me.

I realize I need to be connected and seek guidance from within.

As I become more attune with the Universe, I then become a positive creator of my own experience.

This state of being attracts endless possibilities.

The Universe is infinite and so am I.

The Image: Hoag's Object

A nearly perfect ring of hot, blue stars pinwheels about the yellow nucleus of an unusual galaxy known as Hoag's Object. This image from NASA's Hubble Space Telescope captures a face-on view of the galaxy's ring of stars, revealing more detail than any existing photo of this object. The image may help astronomers unravel clues on how such strange objects form.

The entire galaxy is about 120,000 light-years wide, which is slightly larger than our Milky Way Galaxy. The blue ring, which is dominated by clusters of young, massive stars, contrasts sharply with the yellow nucleus of mostly older stars. What appears to be a "gap" separating the two stellar populations may actually contain some star clusters that are almost too faint to see. Curiously, an object that bears an uncanny resemblance to Hoag's Object can be seen in the gap at the one o'clock position. The object is probably a background ring galaxy.

Photo and description courtesy of Hubblesite.org
Image Credit: NASA and The Hubble Heritage Team (STScI/AURA)
Acknowledgment: Ray A. Lucas (STScI/AURA)

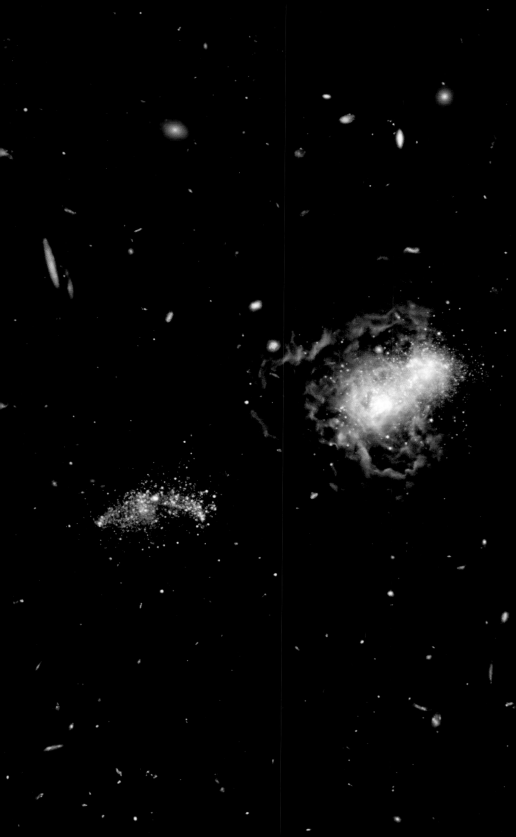

GROWTH

This world is my home.
The Universe is my back yard, and there is plenty of space for me to grow and change.

AFFIRMATIONS

My roots are upon this planet and my vision is beyond.

I am not here by accident.

I have a creative purpose to my life.

As I change, adapt, grow, and explore the unknown, I will then go beyond what I see as possible.

The Image: I Zwicky 18

NASA's Hubble Space Telescope quashed the possibility that what was previously believed to be a toddler galaxy in the nearby universe may actually be considered an adult. Called I Zwicky 18, this galaxy has a youthful appearance that resembles galaxies typically found only in the early universe. Hubble has now found faint, older stars within this galaxy, suggesting that the galaxy may have formed at the same time as most other galaxies.

Photo and description courtesy of Hubblesite.org
Image Credit: NASA, ESA, and A. Aloisi (Space Telescope Science Institute and European Space Agency, Baltimore, MD).

UNIVERSAL CONNECTION

The awe and wonder of the Universe is within me and connects me with all living creatures.

AFFIRMATIONS

A fundamental truth of the Universe is that we are pure energy.

As the Universe expands, my heart expands.

I open my heart and mind and feel the connecting force.

We are a divine family and love binds us together.

The Image: M104

The Sombrero galaxy, Messier 104 (M104) is a brilliant white, bulbous core encircled by the thick dust lanes comprising the spiral structure of the galaxy. As seen from Earth, the galaxy is tilted nearly edge-on. We view it from just six degrees north of its equatorial plane. This brilliant galaxy was named the Sombrero because of its resemblance to the broad rim and high-topped Mexican hat.

At a relatively bright magnitude of +8, M104 is just beyond the limit of naked-eye visibility and is easily seen through small telescopes. The Sombrero lies at the southern edge of the rich Virgo cluster of galaxies and is one of the most massive objects in that group, equivalent to 800 billion suns. The galaxy is 50,000 light-years across and is located 28 million light-years from Earth.

Photo and description courtesy of Hubblesite.org
Image Type: Astronomical
Image Credit: NASA and The Hubble Heritage Team (STScI/AURA)

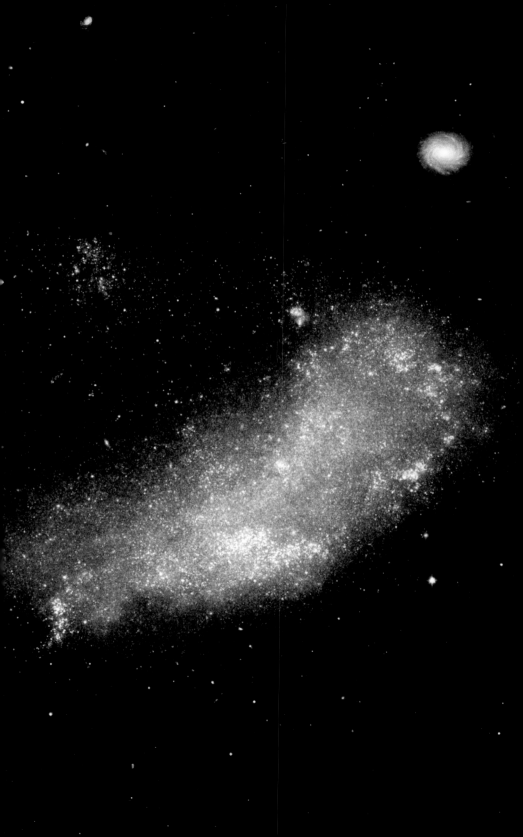

B R E A T H

Breath is the basis of life, as I breathe in the power from Source;
I know I have eternal life.

AFFIRMATIONS

Take a deep breath then exhale slowly. Feel your energy awaken to your personal power.
Bring the blessings of energy into yourself.
Feel the connection with the Universe and know the eternal forces are within.
Become centered in peace.

The Image: NGC 1427A

NGC 1427A, which is located some 62 million light-years away from Earth in the direction of the constellation Fornax, shows numerous hot, blue stars in this image obtained by the Hubble Space Telescope. These blue stars have been formed very recently, showing that star formation is occurring extensively throughout the galaxy.

Galaxy clusters, like the Fornax cluster, contain hundreds or even thousands of individual galaxies. Within the Fornax cluster, there is a considerable amount of gas lying between the galaxies. When the gas within NGC 1427A collides with the Fornax gas, it is compressed to the point that it starts to collapse under its own gravity. This leads to formation of the myriad of new stars seen across NGC 1427A, which give the galaxy an overall arrowhead shape that appears to point in the direction of the galaxy's high-velocity motion. The tidal forces of nearby galaxies in the cluster may also play a role in triggering star formation on such a massive scale.

Photo and description courtesy of Hubblesite.org
Image Credit: NASA, ESA, and The Hubble Heritage Team (STScI/AURA)
Acknowledgment: M. Gregg (Univ. Calif.-Davis and Inst. for Geophysics and Planetary Physics, Lawrence Livermore Natl. Lab.)

COSMIC PULL

As gravity gives the Universe order, the Divine Presence
gives order to my life.

AFFIRMATION

The great bodies of the Universe have an attraction to each other. Everything with mass exerts a force on everything else with mass. Within my heart, the closer I get to Source the stronger the pull of love.

The Image: NGC-1672

This NASA Hubble Space Telescope view of the nearby barred spiral galaxy NGC 1672 unveils details in the galaxy's star-forming clouds and dark bands of interstellar dust. One of the most striking features is the dust lanes that extend away from the nucleus and follow the inner edges of the galaxy's spiral arms. Clusters of hot young blue stars form along the spiral arms and ionize surrounding clouds of hydrogen gas that glow red. Delicate curtains of dust partially obscure and redden the light of the stars behind them by scattering blue light.

Galaxies lying behind NGC 1672 give the illusion they are embedded in the foreground galaxy, even though they are really much farther away. They also appear reddened as they shine through NGC 1672's dust. A few bright foreground stars inside our own Milky Way Galaxy appear in the image as bright and diamond-like objects.

Photo and description courtesy of Hubblesite.org
Image Credit: NASA, ESA, and The Hubble Heritage Team (STScI/AURA)-ESA/Hubble Collaboration

ABUNDANCE

My world is like the ocean, full of abundance. I am in tune with its rhythm,
I flow with its ebb and tide.

AFFIRMATIONS

I am a wonderful and powerful Creator.

I can reach out and attract what is important to me.

There are no limits to the abundance of the Universe.

I am here to create the life I desire.

My thinking is the key.

The Image: Manym Galaxy—Abell-1689

NASA's Hubble and Spitzer space telescopes, with a boost from a natural
"zoom lens," have uncovered what may be one of the youngest and brightest
galaxies ever seen in the middle of the cosmic "dark ages," just 700 million
years after the beginning of our universe.

The distant galaxy, dubbed A1689-zD1, appears as a grayish-white smudge
in the close-up view taken with Hubble's NICMOS [center, right], and as a
whitish blob in the Spitzer IRAC close-up view [bottom, right]. The galaxy is
brimming with star birth. Hubble and Spitzer worked together to show that
it is one of the youngest galaxies ever discovered. Astronomers estimate
that the galaxy is 12.8 billion light-years away. Abell 1689 is 2.2 billion light-
years away.

Photo and description courtesy of Hubblesite.org
Image Credit: NASA, ESA, L. Bradley (JHU), R. Bouwens (UCSC), H. Ford (JHU), and G. Illingworth (UCSC)

VISIONS

I envision my world, and I know that I
create it with mine and God's plan.

AFFIRMATIONS

I choose happiness over hardship.
I release what no longer serves me.
I see the spiritual being I am and my vision is of something great.
My sight is on a new world of oneness and peace.

The Image: M-82

To celebrate the Hubble Space Telescope's 16 years of success, the two space agencies involved in the project, NASA and the European Space Agency (ESA), released this image of the magnificent starburst galaxy, Messier 82 (M82). This mosaic image is the sharpest wide-angle view ever obtained of M82. The galaxy is remarkable for its bright blue disk, webs of shredded clouds, and fiery-looking plumes of glowing hydrogen blasting out of its central regions.

Throughout the galaxy's center, young stars are being born 10 times faster than they are inside our entire Milky Way Galaxy. The resulting huge concentration of young stars carved into the gas and dust at the galaxy's center. The fierce galactic superwind generated from these stars compresses enough gas to make millions of more stars.

Photo and description courtesy of Hubblesite.org
Image Credit: NASA, ESA, and The Hubble Heritage Team (STScI/AURA)
Acknowledgment: J. Gallagher (University of Wisconsin), M. Mountain (STScI), and P. Puxley (National Science Foundation)

GUARDIANS

I am surrounded by many angels,
protecting me with ever step I take.

AFFIRMATIONS

I know I am not alone.

I am guided by angels.

They may come from the spirit world or the world of form.

People I meet on the street, work with, or even live with may be angels in disguise.

May I always remember them and realize I may be an angel to others.

The Image: Ring Galaxy AM-0644-741

Resembling a diamond-encrusted bracelet, a ring of brilliant blue star clusters wraps around the yellowish nucleus of what was once a normal spiral galaxy in this image from NASA's Hubble Space Telescope (HST). The sparkling blue ring is 150,000 light-years in diameter, making it larger than our entire home galaxy, the Milky Way. The galaxy, cataloged as AM 0644-741, is a member of the class of so-called "ring galaxies." It lies 300 million light-years away in the direction of the southern constellation Volans.

Photo and description courtesy of Hubblesite.org
Image Credit: NASA, ESA, and The Hubble Heritage Team (AURA/STScI)
Acknowledgment: J. Higdon (Cornell U.) and I. Jordan (STScI)

BE PRESENT

I am conscious in this moment and know
I am in the presence of Divine Spirit.

AFFIRMATIONS

I do not think of the past or what is in the future.
I live in the moment and feel bliss.
My joy is a compelling aspect of my being.
I do not wait for joy to come into my life, but feel joy NOW.

The Image: M-64

A collision of two galaxies has left a merged star system with an unusual appearance as well as bizarre internal motions. Messier 64 (M64) has a spectacular dark band of absorbing dust in front of the galaxy's bright nucleus, giving rise to its nicknames of the "Black Eye" or "Evil Eye" galaxy.

Photo and description courtesy of Hubblesite.org
Image Credit: NASA and The Hubble Heritage Team (AURA/STScI)
Acknowledgment: S. Smartt (Institute of Astronomy) and D. Richstone (U. Michigan)

TRUST

The hand of God guides me. I trust Him as He leads me to where He has always been.

AFFIRMATIONS

I rely on Source to guide me with love and wisdom.

I know I can trust His guidance.

I open my heart and reach out to Him.

I take His hand and follow Him on my next step back into oneness.

The Image: NGC 2207-NGC 2163

In the direction of the constellation Canis Major, two spiral galaxies pass by each other like majestic ships in the night. The larger and more massive galaxy is cataloged as NGC 2207 (on the left in the Hubble Heritage image), and the smaller one on the right is IC 2163. Strong tidal forces from NGC 2207 have distorted the shape of IC 2163, flinging out stars and gas into long streamers stretching out a hundred thousand light-years toward the right-hand edge of the image.

Photo and description courtesy of Hubblesite.org
Image Credit: NASA, ESA, and The Hubble Heritage Team (STScI)

Inner Light

I follow my inner star, for as I carry my light I then become a
glowing example of light and love.

Affirmations

Being one with Source, I am a vessel of love and light. I then become
a beacon of light to others.

We glow with the light of the Creator.

We see each other through the vision given by God.

This light is unlimited and gives us true life.

The Image: 2MASX

Hubble captures a rare alignment between two spiral galaxies. The outer rim
of a small, foreground galaxy is silhouetted in front of a larger background
galaxy. Skeletal tentacles of dust can be seen extending beyond the
small galaxy's disk of starlight. Such outer dark dusty structures, which
appear to be devoid of stars, like barren branches, are rarely so visible in
a galaxy because there is usually nothing behind them to illuminate them.
Astronomers have never seen dust this far beyond the visible edge of a
galaxy. They do not know if these dusty structures are common features
in galaxies.

Photo and description courtesy of Hubblesite.org
Image Credit: NASA, ESA, and The Hubble Heritage Team (STScI/AURA)
Acknowledgment: B. Holwerda (Space Telescope Science Institute) and J. Dalcanton (University of Washington)

PEACE

I am at peace with myself, and I know that a powerful
presence is working through me.

AFFIRMATIONS

As I experience vibrations from Source, I am in a state of acceptance.

Peace is that subtle calm energy that vibrates within.

I am quiet and still everyday and listen to the voice of my Higher Power.

The Image: Galaxy grouping — Seylerts sextet

The Seyfert's Sextet is a grouping of galaxies engaging in a slow dance of
destruction that will last for billions of years. The galaxies are so tightly packed
together that gravitational forces are beginning to rip stars from them and
distort their shapes. Those same gravitational forces eventually could bring
the galaxies together to form one large galaxy. The name of this grouping,
Seyfert's Sextet, implies that six galaxies are participating in the action. But
only four galaxies are on the dance card. The small face-on spiral with the
prominent arms [center] of gas and stars is a background galaxy almost
five times farther away than the other four. Only a chance alignment makes
it appear as if it is part of the group. The sixth member of the sextet isn't a
galaxy at all but a long "tidal tail" of stars.

Photo and description courtesy of Hubblesite.org
Image Credit: NASA, J. English (U. Manitoba), S. Hunsberger, S. Zonak, J. Charlton, S. Gallagher (PSU), and L. Frattare
(STScI)

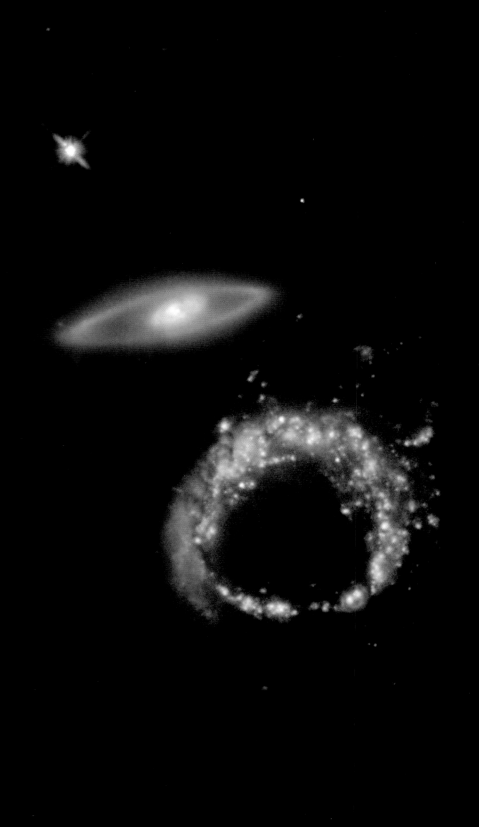

I Am Protected

The Angel of Light protects and guides me along my worldly path.
I am never alone.

Affirmations

I let go of all my worries and relax.

I feel the light of the angels surround me and keep me safe.

I know I have nothing to fear and all I have to do is call on my angels to assist me in whatever area of life I need help. All I have to do is ask.

As I become filled with my angel's energy, I know I am always protected.

I call to my angels every day and keep them close.

 TOP

The Image: Arp-147

The two galaxies happen to be oriented so that they appear to mark the number 10. The left-most galaxy, or the "one" in this image, is relatively undisturbed apart from a smooth ring of starlight. It appears nearly on edge to our line of sight. The right-most galaxy, resembling a zero, exhibits a clumpy, blue ring of intense star formation. The blue ring was most probably formed after the galaxy on the left passed through the galaxy on the right. Just as a pebble thrown into a pond creates an outwardly moving circular wave, a propagating density wave was generated at the point of impact and spread outward. As this density wave collided with material in the target galaxy that was moving inward due to the gravitational pull of the two galaxies, shocks and dense gas were produced, stimulating star formation.

Photo and description courtesy of Hubblesite.org
Image Credit: NASA, ESA, and M. Livio (ST)

SHINING STAR

As a spiritual being I know my light shines brighter than
any star in the Universe.

AFFIRMATIONS

As I look up at the stars I see all the magnificence of the Universe.

I see great potential in each and every human being.

A door is open for celestial guidance, growth, and inspiration.

God's love is always with me and I am never alone.

The Image: M-7

Messier 74, also called NGC 628, is a stunning example of a "grand-design"
spiral galaxy that is viewed by Earth observers nearly face-on. Its perfectly
symmetrical spiral arms emanate from the central nucleus and are dotted with
clusters of young blue stars and glowing pink regions of ionized hydrogen
(hydrogen atoms that have lost their electrons). These regions of star
formation show an excess of light at ultraviolet wavelengths. Tracing along
the spiral arms are winding dust lanes that also begin very near the galaxy's
nucleus and follow along the length of the spiral arms. M74 is located roughly
32 million light-years away in the direction of the constellation Pisces, the Fish.
It is the dominant member of a small group of about half a dozen galaxies,
the M74 galaxy group. In its entirety, it is estimated that M74 is home to about
100 billion stars, making it slightly smaller than our Milky Way.

Photo and description courtesy of Hubblesite.org
Image Credit: NASA, ESA, and the Hubble Heritage (STScI/AURA)-ESA/Hubble Collaboration
Acknowledgment: R. Chandar (University of Toledo) and J. Miller (University of Michigan)

SEEKER

I am a persistent seeker of truth, wisdom, and knowledge,
and the door is always open.

AFFIRMATIONS

In my quest for knowledge about the Universe, I hear Him speak to me.

I desire to awaken to the knowledge of how great God and Spirit are.

I am one with the Universal mind.

May I always remain on this endless adventure.

The Image: M81

This beautiful galaxy is tilted at an oblique angle on to our line of sight, giving a "birds-eye view" of the spiral structure. The galaxy is similar to our Milky Way, but our favorable view provides a better picture of the typical architecture of spiral galaxies. Though the galaxy is 11.6 million light-years away, NASA Hubble Space Telescope's view is so sharp that it can resolve individual stars, along with open star clusters, globular star clusters, and even glowing regions of fluorescent gas.

The spiral arms, which wind all the way down into the nucleus, are made up of young, bluish, hot stars formed in the past few million years. They also host a population of stars formed in an episode of star formation that started about 600 million years ago. The greenish regions are dense areas of bright star formation. The ultraviolet light from hot young stars are fluorescing the surrounding clouds of hydrogen gas. A number of sinuous dust lanes also wind all the way into the nucleus of M81.

Photo and descriptions courtesy of Hubblesite.org
Image Credit: NASA, ESA, and The Hubble Heritage Team (STScI/AURA)

QUIET MEDITATION

When I close my eyes and withdraw from the world around me,
I enter the world of eternal life.

AFFIRMATIONS

As I focus on the internal world, my attention is on the energy field that connects the two worlds, one of spirit and of form.

I feel myself in the past and future, across the Universe, boundless.

As I allow the Divine forces to work through me, I have absolute power, and that power lies within.

The Image: NGC-5866

Hubble's sharp vision reveals a crisp dust lane dividing the galaxy into two halves. The image highlights the galaxy's structure: a subtle, reddish bulge surrounding a bright nucleus, a blue disk of stars running parallel to the dust lane, and a transparent outer halo.

Some faint, wispy trails of dust can be seen meandering away from the disk of the galaxy out into the bulge and inner halo of the galaxy. The outer halo is dotted with numerous gravitationally bound clusters of nearly a million stars each, known as globular clusters. Background galaxies that are millions to billions of light-years farther away than NGC 5866 are also seen through the halo.

Photo and description courtesy of Hubblesite.org
Image Credit: NASA, ESA, and The Hubble Heritage Team (STScI/AURA)
Acknowledgment: W. Keel (University of Alabama, Tuscaloosa)

ENCHANTMENT

The Universe is magical.
It creates wonderful miracles in my world.

AFFIRMATIONS

The Universe holds an abundant supply of adventure.

Source is generous and provides me with a rich life full of blessings.

The Universe gives me wisdom and a control of unseen forces that can operate in my life.

He reveals secret knowledge that will lead me to my power.

I prosper from Divine power.

The Image: Galaxy cluster MACS-J0717

This composite image shows the massive galaxy cluster MACS J0717.5+3745 (MACS J0717, for short), where four separate galaxy clusters have been involved in a collision – the first time such a phenomenon has been documented. The repeated collisions in MACS J0717 are caused by a 13-million-light-year-long stream of galaxies, gas, and dark matter – known as a filament – pouring into a region already full of matter. A collision between the gases in two or more clusters causes the hot gas to slow down. However, the massive and compact galaxies do not slow down as much as the gas does, and so move ahead of it. Therefore, the speed and direction of each cluster's motion – perpendicular to the line of sight – can be estimated by studying the offset between the average position of the galaxies and the peak in the hot gas. MACS J0717 is located about 5.4 billion light-years from Earth. It is one of the most complex galaxy clusters ever seen.

Photo and description courtesy of Hubblesite.org
Image Credit: NASA, ESA, CXC, C. Ma, H. Ebeling, and E. Barrett (University of Hawaii/IfA), et al., and STScI

CELESTIAL MUSIC

As I hear the angels sing their songs of love,
I am in tune with their melodies.

AFFIRMATIONS

Love is the song of the angels. They sing their pure notes in the symphony of the Universe.

Their tunes are magnetic and draw me in.

They vibrate like the strings of Celestial violins.

As I add my voice to the chorus, I am in unison.

The Image: Abell 1656

Known as Abell 1656, the Coma Cluster is over 300 million light-years away. The cluster, named after its parent constellation, Coma Berenices, is near the Milky Way's north pole. This places the Coma Cluster in an area unobscured by dust and gas from the plane of the Milky Way, and easily visible by Earth viewers. Most of the galaxies that inhabit the central portion of the Coma Cluster are ellipticals. These featureless "fuzz-balls" are pale goldish-brown in color and contain populations of old stars. Both dwarf, as well as giant ellipticals, are found in abundance in the Coma Cluster.

Farther out from the center of the cluster are several spiral galaxies. These galaxies have clouds of cold gas that are giving birth to new stars. Spiral arms and dust lanes "accessorize" these bright bluish-white galaxies that show a distinctive disk structure.

Photo and description courtesy of Hubblesite.org
Image Credit: NASA, ESA, and the Hubble Heritage Team (STScI/AURA)
Acknowledgment: D. Carter (Liverpool John Moores University) and the Coma HST ACS Treasury Team

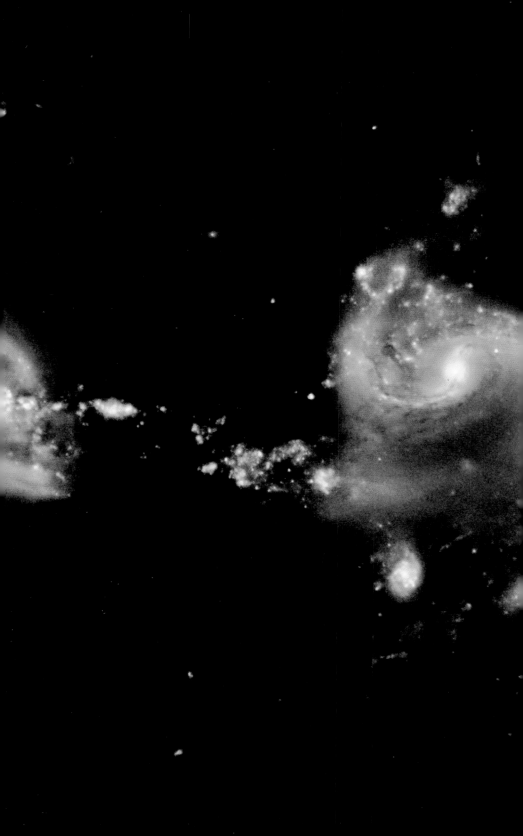

Divine Guidance

I am secure in the knowledge of my place in the Universe.
I allow Divine guidance to school me.

Affirmations

I am made from God; God is in me.

One energy flows through us.

I am larger then I know.

He imbues me with love, He gives me his power, and He teaches me goodness.

I am thankful and alert to the abundance of the Universe.

The Image: Arp 194

This interacting group contains several galaxies, along with a "cosmic fountain" of stars, gas, and dust that stretches over 100,000 light-years. The northern (upper) component of Arp 194 appears as a haphazard collection of dusty spiral arms, bright blue star-forming regions, and at least two galaxy nuclei that appear to be connected and in the early stages of merging. A third, relatively normal, spiral galaxy appears off to the right. The southern (lower) component of the galaxy group contains a single large spiral galaxy with its own blue star-forming regions. However, the most striking feature of this galaxy troupe is the impressive blue stream of material extending from the northern component. This "fountain" contains complexes of super star clusters, each one of which may contain dozens of individual young star clusters. The blue color is produced by the hot, massive stars which dominate the light in each cluster. Overall, the "fountain" contains many millions of stars.

Photo and description courtesy of Hubblesite.org
Image Credit: NASA, ESA, and the Hubble Heritage Team (STScI/AURA)

CELESTIAL GUIDANCE

I am a master astrologer; I follow the stars knowing
His grace, love, and protection.

AFFIRMATIONS

As I gaze into the night sky and see the stars in all their glory, I feel the expressions of great wonder as the stars beckon me.

The cosmic rhythms bring me new opportunities and experiences for self knowledge.

They offer me security and refuge as they carry me towards my spiritual destiny.

The Image: Abell S0740

A collection of galaxies in the cluster Abell S0740 that is over 450 million light-years away in the direction of the constellation Centaurus. The giant elliptical ESO 325-G004 looms large at the cluster's center. The galaxy is as massive as 100 billion of our suns. Hubble resolves thousands of globular star clusters orbiting ESO 325-G004. Globular clusters are compact groups of hundreds of thousands of stars that are gravitationally bound together. At the galaxy's distance they appear as pinpoints of light contained within the diffuse halo.

Other fuzzy elliptical galaxies dot the image. Some have evidence of a disk or ring structure that gives them a bow-tie shape. Several spiral galaxies are also present. The starlight in these galaxies is mainly contained in a disk and follows along spiral arms.

Photo and description courtesy of Hubblesite.org
Image Credit: NASA, ESA, and The Hubble Heritage Team (STScI/AURA)
Acknowledgment: J. Blakeslee (Washington State University)

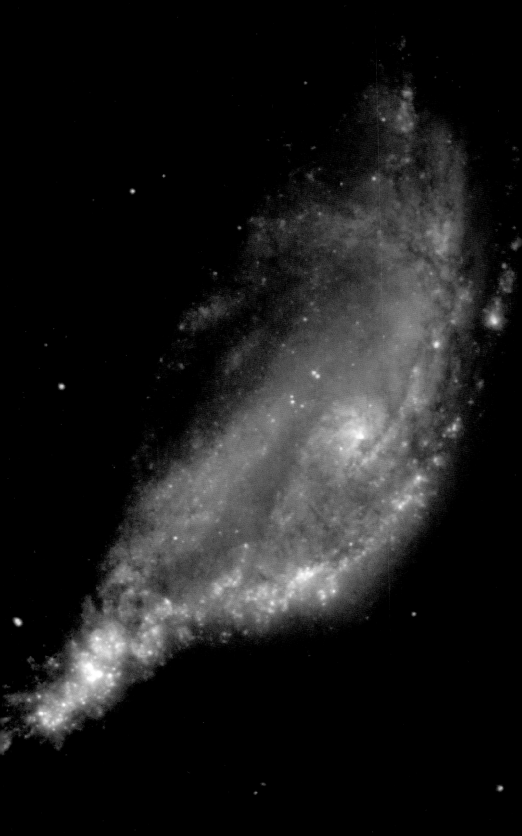

ANSWERS

I need only to have faith and believe
and the answers will be there.

AFFIRMATIONS

I call upon the Universe to ask for direction and help.
God is my source and I embrace His wisdom.
I welcome and receive His support.
He is my counselor and I am always heard.

The Image: NGC-6745

What appears as a bird's head, leaning over to snatch up a tasty meal, is a striking example of a galaxy collision in NGC 6745. A large spiral galaxy, with its nucleus still intact, peers at the smaller passing galaxy (nearly out of the field of view at lower right), while a bright blue beak and bright whitish-blue top feathers show the distinct path taken during the smaller galaxy's journey. These galaxies did not merely interact gravitationally as they passed one another, they actually collided.

When galaxies collide, the stars that normally comprise the major portion of the luminous mass of each of the two galaxies will almost never collide with each other, but will pass rather freely between each other with little damage. This occurs because the physical size of individual stars is tiny compared to their typical separations, making the chance of physical encounter relatively small. In our own Milky Way galaxy, the space between our Sun and our nearest stellar neighbor, Proxima Centauri (part of the Alpha Centauri triple system), is a vast 4.3 light-years.

Photo and description courtesy of Hubblesite.org
Image Credit: NASA and The Hubble Heritage Team (STScI/AURA)
Acknowledgment: Roger Lynds (KPNO/NOAO)

THE LAW OF ATTRACTION

Through the law of attraction,
all I ever choose comes to me.

AFFIRMATIONS

I am a powerful magnate.
I carefully choose my thoughts and feelings and the Universe brings to me whatever I desire.
I am the creator of my own reality.
I have no limits.

The Image: NGC-3949

Our Sun and solar system are embedded in a broad pancake of stars deep within the disk of the Milky Way galaxy. Even from a distance, it is impossible to see our galaxy's large-scale features other than the disk. NGC 3949 lies about 50 million light-years from Earth. It is a member of a loose cluster of some six or seven dozens of galaxies located in the direction of the Big Dipper, in the constellation Ursa Major (the Great Bear). It is one of the larger galaxies of this cluster.

Photo and description courtesy of NASA.gov and Hubblesite.org
Image Credit: NASA/ESA/Hubble Heritage Team

TRUST

I know the love of God supplies me with faith
and trust in life's processes.

AFFIRMATIONS

I accept the guidance that comes from the All Knowing.

I know that by His love, He guides me well and keeps me safe.

In every moment of perceived darkness, He has been there with me.

I open my heart and mind to the power of the Universe, as He is committed to my purpose.

The Image: M51

The graceful, winding arms of the majestic spiral galaxy M51 (NGC 5194) appear like a grand spiral staircase sweeping through space. They are actually long lanes of stars and gas laced with dust. The Whirlpool's most striking feature is its two curving arms, a hallmark of so-called grand-design spiral galaxies. Many spiral galaxies possess numerous, loosely shaped arms which make their spiral structure less pronounced. These arms serve an important purpose in spiral galaxies. They are star-formation factories, compressing hydrogen gas and creating clusters of new stars. In the Whirlpool, the assembly line begins with the dark clouds of gas on the inner edge, then moves to bright pink star-forming regions, and ends with the brilliant blue star clusters along the outer edge.

Photo and description courtesy of Hubblesite.org
Image **Credit:** [Whirlpool Galaxy] - NASA, ESA, S. Beckwith (STScI), and The Hubble Heritage Team (STScI/AURA) [Eagle Nebula] - NASA, ESA, and The Hubble Heritage Team (STScI/AURA)

Awareness

As I become more aware of my inner nature,
I become more aware of the spiritual vibrations of others.

Affirmations

As I connect to my Higher power, I become filled with His presence.
I then feel the connection with other souls.
My source is everyone's source.
My power is everyone's power.
My heart is everyone's heart.
We are sourced in Divine goodness.
We are unique souls and creative goodness is our true nature.

The Image: Crab Nebula M-1

This is a mosaic image of the Crab Nebula, a six-light-year-wide expanding remnant of a star's supernova explosion. Japanese and Chinese astronomers recorded this violent event nearly 1,000 years ago in 1054, as did, almost certainly, Native Americans.

The orange filaments are the tattered remains of the star and consist mostly of hydrogen. The rapidly spinning neutron star embedded in the center of the nebula is the dynamo powering the nebula's eerie interior bluish glow. The blue light comes from electrons whirling at nearly the speed of light around magnetic field lines from the neutron star. The neutron star, like a lighthouse, ejects twin beams of radiation that appear to pulse 30 times a second due to the neutron star's rotation. A neutron star is the crushed ultra-dense core of the exploded star.

Photo and description courtesy of Hubblesite.org
Image Credit: NASA, ESA, J. Hester and A. Loll (Arizona State University)

DREAM MAKER

The Universe blends everything in a harmonious way.
My dreams and desires are sustained by Divine power.

AFFIRMATIONS

I walk in spiritual oneness; my companion is the Creator.
He is the benevolent force that comes to me from all directions.
He sees that my dreams come true.
He sees that my works are accomplished.
The blending of His love and counsel, make my life complete.

The Image: Light Echo

Hubble Space Telescope views of an unusual phenomenon in space called a light echo. Light from a star that erupted nearly five years ago continues propagating outward through a cloud of dust surrounding the star. The light reflects or "echoes" off the dust and then travels to Earth.

Because of the extra distance the scattered light travels, it reaches the Earth long after the light from the stellar outburst itself. Therefore, a light echo is an analog of a sound echo produced, for example, when sound from an Alpine yodeler echoes off of the surrounding mountainsides.

The echo comes from the unusual variable star V838 Monocerotis (V838 Mon), located 20,000 light-years away on the periphery of our Galaxy. In early 2002, V838 Mon increased in brightness temporarily to become 600,000 times brighter than our Sun. The reason for the eruption is still unclear.

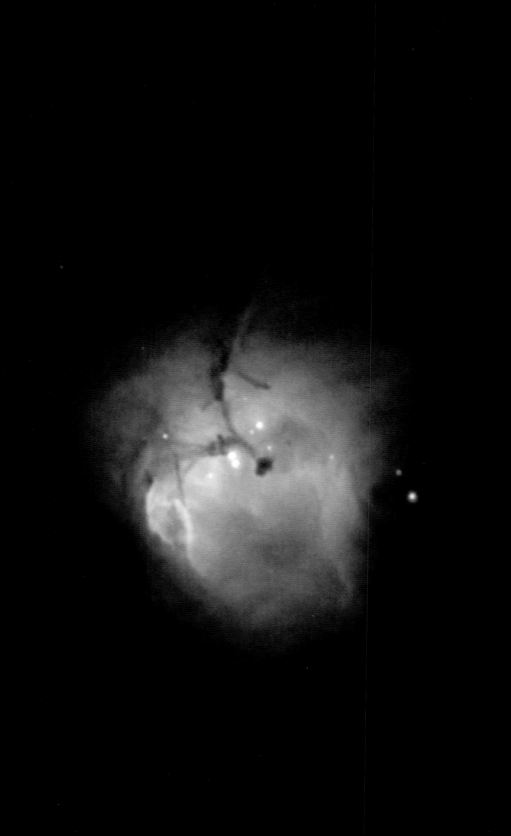

My Guardian Angel

My angel is always standing by, waiting for me to appeal to his wisdom and turn to him for counsel.

AFFIRMATIONS

I am blessed by counsel in many ways.
I am divinely loved and lead.
I cherish my companions and their tender love as they hold me in safety.
I surrender to higher forces as they mentor me towards my dreams.

The Image: Small Magellanic Cloud N-81

NASA's Hubble Space Telescope has peered deep into a neighboring galaxy to reveal details of the formation of new stars. Hubble's target was a newborn star cluster within the Small Magellanic Cloud, a small galaxy that is a satellite of our own Milky Way. The new images show young, brilliant stars cradled within a nebula, or glowing cloud of gas, cataloged as N 81.

These massive, recently formed stars inside N 81 are losing material at a high rate, sending out strong stellar winds and shock waves and hollowing out a cocoon within the surrounding nebula. The two most luminous stars, seen in the Hubble image as a very close pair near the center of N 81, emit copious ultraviolet radiation, causing the nebula to glow through fluorescence.

SPIRIT GUIDES

I am guided by many spiritual companions;
they quietly lead me on my life's journey.

AFFIRMATIONS

There are others who are with me on my journey.

There are many who walk with me from the spirit world.

I feel their presence as they guide and protect me.

They communicate with me without words.

They are beings from the higher realms and there is much insight gained from them.

The Image: Nubula SuWt2

This image of the planetary nebula SuWt 2 reveals a bright ring-like structure encircling a bright central star. The central star is actually a close binary system where two stars completely circle each other every five days. The interaction of these stars and the more massive star that sheds material to create the nebula formed the ring structure. The burned out core of the massive companion has yet to be found inside the nebula. The nebula is located 6,500 light-years from Earth in the direction of the constellation Centaurus.

Photo and description courtesy of Hubblesite.org
Image Credit: NASA, NOAO, H. Bond and K. Exter (STScI/AURA)

GRATITUDE

With the help of the Universe, I reach my goals
and I give thanks for the guidance.

AFFIRMATIONS

God is the source of all my achievements.

The Creator has given me support and divine aid.

All my blessings come from Him.

How can I go through life and not thank Him for all He has given me?

I am thankful and grateful for the beauty He has bestowed on me.

I count my many blessings.

The Image: NGC 4319 — Markarian 205

NGC 4319 is 80 million light-years from Earth. Markarian 205 (Mrk 205) is more than 14 times farther away, residing 1 billion light-years from Earth. The apparent close alignment of Mrk 205 and NGC 4319 is simply a matter of chance. Astronomers used two methods to determine the distances to these objects. First, they measured how their light has been stretched in space due to the universe's expansion. Then they measured how much the ultraviolet light from Mrk 205 dimmed as it passed through the interstellar gas of NGC 4319.

At a distance of 1 billion light-years, Mrk 205 is a relatively nearby quasar. Many quasars reside much farther away. Quasars, once known only as mysterious point-like objects, are now known to be distant galaxies that have extremely bright cores. These powerhouses of light are probably fueled by massive black holes. With powerful telescopes like Hubble, it is often possible to see the quasar's surrounding halo of faint starlight, as is clearly visible around Mrk 205.

Photo and description courtesy of Hubblesite.org
Credits: NASA and The Hubble Heritage Team (STScI/AURA)
Acknowledgment: R. Knacke (Penn State Erie)

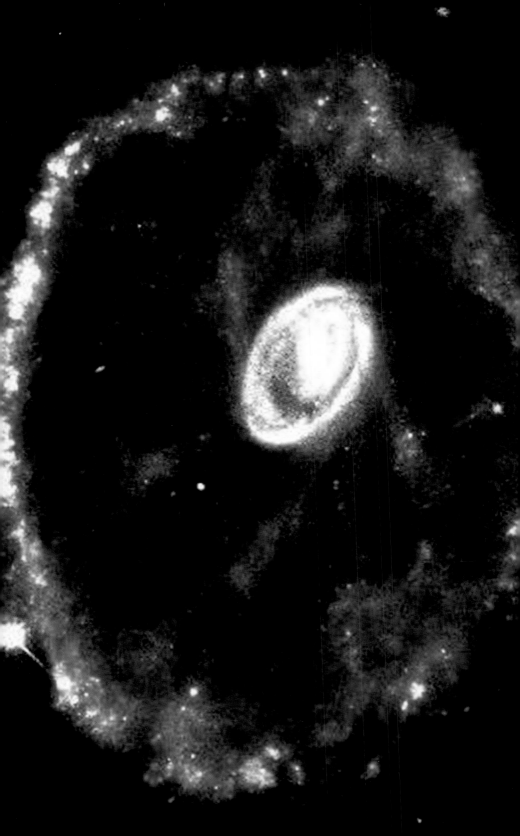

GOD'S GARDEN

I am a flower in the mind of God
and I am rooted in His Divine love.

AFFIRMATIONS

The lilies of the fields are rooted in the earth, and their roots penetrate deep into the soil and receive nourishment. I am deeply rooted in the celestial oneness of the Protector and love is the nourishment I receive.

The Image: A false color view of the Cartwheel Galax

A rare and spectacular head-on collision between two galaxies appears in this NASA Hubble Space Telescope true-color image of the Cartwheel Galaxy, located 500 million light-years away in the constellation Sculptor. The new details of star birth resolved by Hubble provide an opportunity to study how extremely massive stars are born in large fragmented gas clouds.

The Cartwheel Galaxy presumably was a normal spiral galaxy like our Milky Way before the collision. This spiral structure is beginning to re-emerge, as seen in the faint arms or spokes between the outer ring and bulls-eye shaped nucleus. The ring contains at least several billion new stars that would not normally have been created in such a short time span and is so large (150,000 light-years across) our entire Milky Way Galaxy would fit inside.

Photo and description courtesy of Hubblesite.org
Image Credit: Curt Struck and Philip Appleton (Iowa State University), Kirk Borne (Hughes STX Corporation), and Ray Lucas (Space Telescope Science Institute), and NASA

RECEIVING

There are many ways in which the Universe gives me abundance;
I am always open to receive the flow.

AFFIRMATIONS

I open my heart to receiving love and direction.

As I place my trust in the Divine, I draw upon an unlimited supply of success.

The Universe can manifest every dream I dream, every desire I desire.

My success with source is unceasing.

The Image: NGC 1309

Looking like a child's pinwheel ready to be set a spinning by a gentle breeze, this dramatic spiral is cataloged as NGC 1309, are captured in this color image.

Recent observations of the galaxy taken in visible and infrared light come together in a colorful depiction of many of the galaxy's features. Bright blue areas of star formation pepper the spiral arms, while ruddy dust lanes follow the spiral structure into a yellowish central nucleus of older-population stars. The image is complemented by myriad far-off background galaxies.

Photo and description courtesy of Hubblesite.org
Image Credit: NASA, ESA, The Hubble Heritage Team, (STScI/AURA) and A. Riess (STScI)

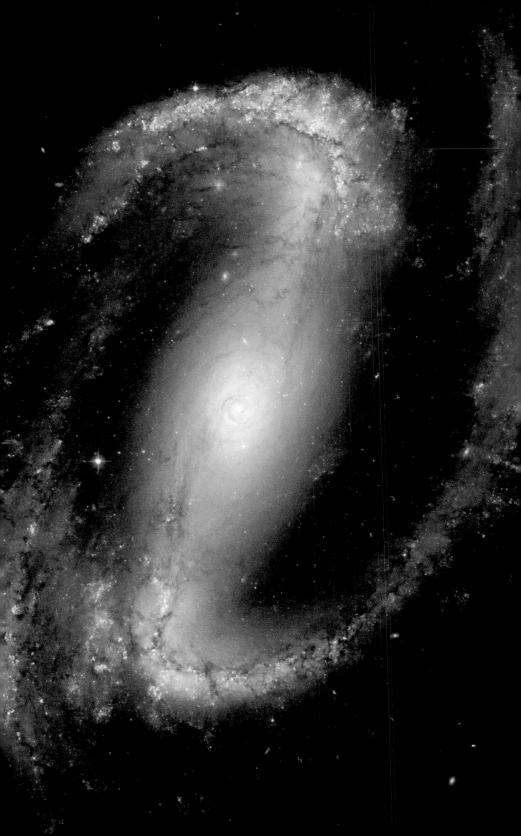

My Rich Life

Mine is an abundant life, full of variety.
Source enriches my life in many ways.

Affirmations

The Universe responds to me.
There are no limitations or boundaries.
All levels of my desire are fulfilled.
I need only to adjust my will and to accept the realization of my dreams.
I honor the gifts and diversity the Universe has supplied me.

The Image: NGC-1300

The Hubble telescope captured a display of starlight, glowing gas, and silhouetted dark clouds of interstellar dust in this 4-foot-by-8-foot image of the barred spiral galaxy NGC 1300. NGC 1300 is considered to be prototypical of barred spiral galaxies. Barred spirals differ from normal spiral galaxies in that the arms of the galaxy do not spiral all the way into the center, but are connected to the two ends of a straight bar of stars containing the nucleus at its center.

Photo and description courtesy of Hubblesite.org
Image Credit: NASA, ESA, and The Hubble Heritage Team (STScI/AURA)

Goodness

I know I am guided by a higher power, and the voice of truth
guides me to all that is good.

AFFIRMATIONS

I hear and listen quietly to the voice of my Creator.

My principles are shaped by my inner knowing.

Goodness is all that He gives me; goodness is all that I give others.

He speaks of eternal life and guides me towards my spiritual success.

 TOP

The Image: NGC 346

This is a Hubble Space Telescope view of one of the most dynamic and
intricately detailed star-forming regions in space, located 210,000 light-
years away in the Small Magellanic Cloud (SMC), a satellite galaxy of our
Milky Way. At the center of the region is a brilliant star cluster called NGC
346. A dramatic structure of arched, ragged filaments with a distinct ridge
surrounds the cluster.

Photo and description courtesy of Hubblesite.org
Image Credit: NASA, ESA, and A. Nota (STScI/ESA)

Change

Change is a permanent law of the Universe.
I am blessed by Source to make my change for the better.

AFFIRMATIONS

I see myself as a work in progress.

I accept Divine help in all areas of my life.

God is the guardian of my soul.

I am guided and empowered as I act for my higher good.

I will recreate a new day and focus on a new dream.

As I change my mind, I am then able to change my life.

The Image: NGC 3314

This image from NASA's Hubble Space Telescope and its Wide Field Planetary Camera 2 (WFPC2) shows the unique galaxy pair called NGC 3314. Through an extraordinary chance alignment, a face-on spiral galaxy lies precisely in front of another larger spiral. This line-up provides us with the rare chance to visualize dark material within the front galaxy, seen only because it is silhouetted against the object behind it NGC 3314 lies about 140 million light-years from Earth, in the direction of the southern hemisphere constellation Hydra. The bright blue stars forming a pinwheel shape near the center of the front galaxy have formed recently from interstellar gas and dust.

Photos and description courtesy of Hubblesite.org
Image Credit: NASA and The Hubble Heritage Team (STScI/AURA)

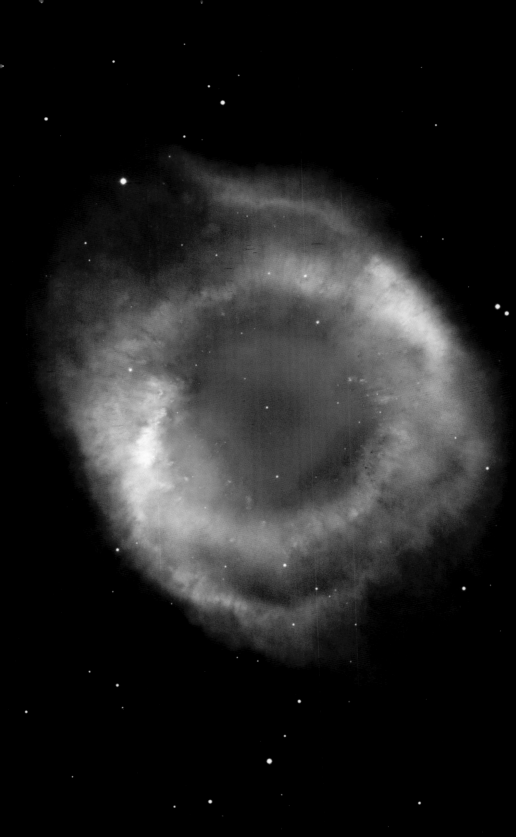

Acceptance

The great spirit of Universal wisdom fills my soul. As I accept the insight and knowledge, I realize my unique potential.

Affirmations

I accept the now and dwell in this state of allowing.

As I shift my thoughts to the oneness of the Universe, I am filled with understanding and wisdom.

I know I have opportunities and support which lead my spirit towards unending powers.

The Image: Helix Nebula NGC 7293

This photograph of the coil-shaped Helix Nebula is one of the largest and most detailed celestial images ever made. The composite picture is a seamless blend of ultra-sharp images from NASA's Hubble Space Telescope combined with the wide view of the Mosaic Camera on the National Science Foundation's 0.9-meter telescope at Kitt Peak National Observatory near Tucson, Arizona. The image shows a fine web of filamentary "bicycle-spoke" features embedded in the colorful red and blue ring of gas. At 650 light-years away, the Helix is one of the nearest planetary nebulae to Earth. A planetary nebula is the glowing gas around a dying, Sun-like star.

Photo and description courtesy of Hubblesite.org
Image Credit: NASA, NOAO, ESA, the Hubble Helix Nebula Team, M. Meixner (STScI), and T.A. Rector (NRAO)

SERVICE

I am an energetic worker and I am willing to serve.
As I serve others I serve my higher power.

AFFIRMATIONS

As I journey through each day with joyous intentions, I bring assistance and pleasure to others.

I look for opportunities to serve, even if it just a smile and a friendly gesture.

I know that as I serve others, I serve my Creator.

The Image: NGC 4414

The Hubble picture shows that the central regions of this galaxy, as is typical of most spirals, contain primarily older, yellow and red stars. The outer spiral arms are considerably bluer due to ongoing formation of young, blue stars, the brightest of which can be seen individually at the high resolution provided by the Hubble camera. The arms are also very rich in clouds of interstellar dust, seen as dark patches and streaks silhouetted against the starlight.

The resulting distance to NGC 4414, 19.1 megaparsecs or about 60 million light-years, along with similarly determined distances to other nearby galaxies, contributes to astronomers' overall knowledge of the rate of expansion of the universe. The Hubble constant (H0) is the ratio of how fast galaxies are moving away from us to their distance from us. This astronomical value is used to determine distances, sizes, and the intrinsic luminosities for many objects in our universe, and the age of the universe itself.

CONNECTION

I am connected to all of life. In everyone I meet I see myself.
We are sourced in Divine Origin. The living Universe dwells within us.

AFFIRMATIONS

I am a spirit among spirits.

I find beauty in my fellow souls.

We are one mind, we are one nature, we are one vision, and we are one heart.

We share each others dreams.

I cherish the kinship of my fellow spirits.

My heart is as expansive as the Universe.

I bless the unity and all it brings.

The Image: Galaxy—NGC 6369

This stellar swarm is M80 (NGC 6093), one of the densest of the 147 known globular star clusters in the Milky Way galaxy. Located about 28,000 light-years from Earth, M80 contains hundreds of thousands of stars, all held together by their mutual gravitational attraction. Globular clusters are particularly useful for studying stellar evolution, since all of the stars in the cluster have the same age (about 15 billion years), but cover a range of stellar masses. Every star visible in this image is either more highly evolved than, or in a few rare cases more massive than, our own Sun. Especially obvious are the bright red giants, which are stars similar to the Sun in mass that are nearing the ends of their lives.

Photo and description courtesy of Hubblesite.org
Image Credit: The Hubble Heritage Team (AURA/ STScI/ NASA)

FAITH

As I study the stars, I see the great wonders of this Universe,
but I am guided by a greater vision and I have faith in His guidance.

AFFIRMATIONS

As I feel the pull of the light in the night sky, I am compelled by what is beyond.

As I look deeper into space, I feel the compassion and benevolence of the Universe.

His compassion overwhelms me.

I have faith that the Universe leads me to privilege and growth.

He gives me hope and guides me to my higher good.

The Image: Galaxy—NGC 2440

This image, taken by NASA's Hubble Space Telescope, shows the colorful "last hurrah" of a star like our Sun. The star is ending its life by casting off its outer layers of gas, which formed a cocoon around the star's remaining core. Ultraviolet light from the dying star makes the material glow. The burned-out star, called a white dwarf, is the white dot in the center. Our Sun will eventually burn out and shroud itself with stellar debris, but not for another 5 billion years.

Photo and description courtesy of Hubblesite.org
Image Credit: NASA, ESA, and K. Noll (STScl)
Acknowledgment: The Hubble Heritage Team (STScl/AURA)

Remember

My destiny is to remember my divinity; my free will
and God's are one and the same.

Affirmations

If we can remember the beings of light and love that we are, then there will be no more
prejudice, judgment, control, sadness, separation, and war.
Today I will REMEMBER.

The Image: NGC 602

This image taken with NASA's Hubble Space Telescope depicts bright, blue,
newly formed stars that are blowing a cavity in the center of a star-forming
region in the Small Magellanic Cloud. At the heart of the star-forming region,
lies star cluster NGC 602. The high-energy radiation blazing out from the hot
young stars is sculpting the inner edge of the outer portions of the nebula,
slowly eroding it away and eating into the material beyond. The diffuse outer
reaches of the nebula prevent the energetic outflows from streaming away
from the cluster.

The Small Magellanic Cloud, in the constellation Tucana, is roughly 200,000
light-years from the Earth. Its proximity to us makes it an exceptional laboratory
to perform in-depth studies of star formation processes and their evolution in
an environment slightly different from our own Milky Way.

Photo and description courtesy of Hubblesite.org
Image Credit: NASA, ESA, and the Hubble Heritage Team (STScI/AURA) - ESA/Hubble Collaboration

DIVINE LIGHT

The light of my spirit glows with His love;
everything is one in this light.

AFFIRMATIONS

As I stand in the center of the Universe, my awareness is on oneness.
My spirit shines with the blessings of the Creator.
His power is in me and I am in His power.
There is one essence that runs through all of us.
I am full of His light.
I glow with the abundance of His power.
The Divine spark shines forth into the Universe.

The Image: NGC 4449

NGC 4449 has been forming stars for several billion years, but currently it is experiencing a star formation event at a much higher rate than in the past. This unusually explosive and intense star formation activity qualifies as a starburst. At the current rate, the gas supply that feeds the stellar production would only last for another billion years or so.

Starbursts usually occur in the central regions of galaxies, but NGC 4449 has more widespread star formation activity, since the very youngest stars are observed both in the nucleus and in streams surrounding the galaxy.

Photo and description courtesy of Hubblesite.org
Image Credit: NASA, ESA, A. Aloisi (STScI/ESA), and The Hubble Heritage (STScI/AURA)-ESA/Hubble Collaboration

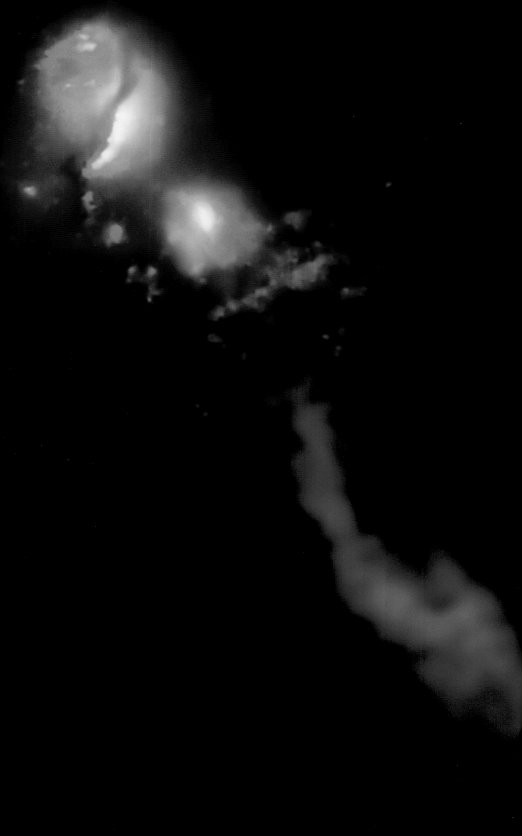

VOICES

As I set in quiet meditation I hear a voice deep within.
I know it is His voice and He speaks with love and truth.

AFFIRMATIONS

As I surrender to where all things are known and understood, I invite the Universe to speak to me.
I welcome thoughts of my Creator as He speaks to me clearly.
I am aware of His silent presence and I respond to His voice as I listen with my heart.

The Image: 3C321

This composite image shows the jet from a black hole at the center of a galaxy striking the edge of another galaxy, the first time such an interaction has been found. In the image, data from several wavelengths have been combined. X-rays from Chandra (colored purple), optical and ultraviolet (UV) data from Hubble (red and orange), and radio emission from the Very Large Array (VLA) and MERLIN (blue) show how the jet from the main galaxy on the lower left is striking its companion galaxy to the upper right. The jet impacts the companion galaxy at its edge and is then disrupted and deflected, much like how a stream of water from a hose will splay out after hitting a wall at an angle.

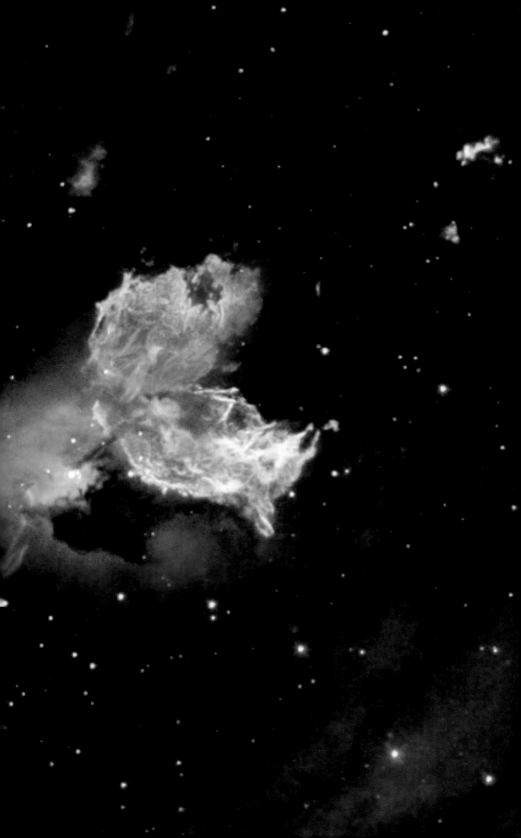

UNIVERSAL WONDERS

I accept love, guidance and peace.
The wonders of the Universe are mine.
May I never lose sight of Source.

AFFIRMATIONS

Today I am choosing to let go of limitation.
I choose to notice the big and little blessings of my life.
I open my heart and choose Divine direction.
I commit myself to the wonderment of His gifts.
I bless the Universe and allow it to guide me.

The Image: Supernove remnant N 63A

A violent and chaotic-looking mass of gas and dust is seen in this Hubble
Space Telescope image of a nearby supernova remnant. Denoted N 63A, the
object is the remains of a massive star that exploded, spewing its gaseous
layers out into an already turbulent region. The supernova remnant is a
member of N 63, a star-forming region in the Large Magellanic Cloud (LMC).
Visible from the southern hemisphere, the LMC is an irregular galaxy lying
160,000 light-years from our own Milky Way galaxy.

Photo and description courtesy of Hubblesite.org
Image Credit: NASA, ESA, HEIC, and The Hubble Heritage Team (STScI/AURA)
Acknowledgment: Y.-H. Chu and R. M. Williams (UIUC)

My Caretaker

My life is like a garden, and as He tends my garden I know my flowers are nourished with peace and love.

Affirmations

I receive direction and help from Source.

My dreams and ambitions are seeds.

He watches over me and sees that I am nurtured.

I am the bud that is ready to blossom, and He is the nourishing rain.

The Image: Star V838

This image, obtained with the Advanced Camera for Surveys on February 8, 2004, is Hubble's view of an expanding halo of light around a distant star, named V838 Monocerotis (V838 Mon). The illumination of interstellar dust comes from the red supergiant star at the middle of the image, which gave off a flashbulb-like pulse of light two years ago. V838 Mon is located about 20,000 light-years away from Earth in the direction of the constellation Monoceros, placing the star at the outer edge of our Milky Way galaxy.

Photo and description courtesy of Hubblesite.org
Image Credit: NASA and The Hubble Heritage Team (AURA/STScI)

GIFTS OF THE SPIRIT

I live in harmony and love;
I feel His divine gifts surround me.

AFFIRMATIONS

As I am embraced with His power, I feel the blessings of the Creator.
He guides, protects, and loves me.
I am secure in His arms.
I open my life to the All Powerful.

The Image: NGC 4038 4039

The Antennae galaxies is the sharpest yet of this merging pair of galaxies. During the course of the collision, billions of stars will be formed. The brightest and most compact of these star birth regions are called super star clusters. The image allows astronomers to better distinguish between the stars and super star clusters created in the collision of two spiral galaxies.

Photo and description courtesy of Hubblesite.org
Image Credit: NASA, ESA, and the Hubble Heritage Team (STScI/AURA)-ESA/Hubble Collaboration
Acknowledgment: B. Whitmore (Space Telescope Science Institute)

A New Day

I leave behind the pain of the past.
I create my new day full of wondrous things.

Affirmations

I release my pain. It is no longer who I am and does not serve me.
I create a new and wonderful life free of obstacles.
My days are expanded, with a new direction and new success.
Today, I am in control of my world.

The Image: NGC 4622

NGC 4622 is a rare example of a spiral galaxy with arms pointing in opposite directions. What caused this galaxy to behave differently from most galaxies? Astronomers suspect that NGC 4622 interacted with another galaxy. Its two outer arms are lopsided, meaning that something disturbed it. The Hubble image suggests that NGC 4622 consumed a small companion galaxy. The galaxy's core provides new evidence for a merger between NGC 4622 and a smaller galaxy. This information could be the key to understanding the unusual leading arms.

Photo and description courtesy of Hubblesite.org
Image Credit: NASA and The Hubble Heritage Team (STScI/AURA)
Acknowledgment: Dr. Ron Buta (U. Alabama), Dr. Gene Byrd (U. Alabama) and Tarsh Freeman (Bevill State Community College)

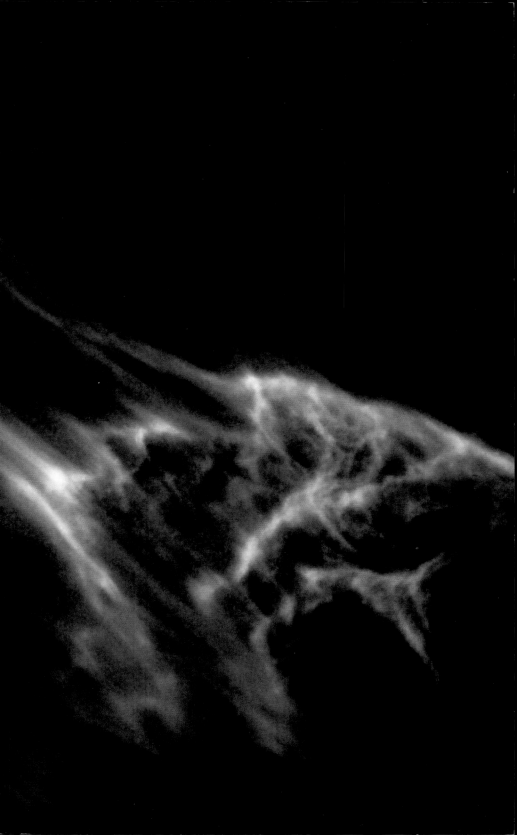

POTENTIAL

I am a spring pouring forth from
the ocean of universal potential.

AFFIRMATIONS

I draw from the ocean of oneness.

I am open to the Universe in all its forms.

It empowers me as I journey through this life as it leads me to a new voyage of discovery.

The Image: Ghostly reflections of the Pleiades

NASA's Hubble Space Telescope has caught the eerie, wispy tendrils of a dark interstellar cloud being destroyed by the passage of one of the brightest stars in the Pleiades star cluster. Like a flashlight beam shining off the wall of a cave, the star is reflecting light off the surface of pitch black clouds of cold gas laced with dust. These are called reflection nebulae.

The famous cluster is easily visible in the evening sky during the winter months as a small grouping of bright blue stars, named after the "Seven Sisters" of Greek mythology. Resembling a small dipper, this star cluster lies in the constellation Taurus at a distance of about 380 light-years from Earth. The unaided eye can discern about half a dozen bright stars in the cluster, but a small telescope will reveal that the Pleiades contains many hundreds of fainter stars.

Photo and description courtesy of Hubblesite.org
Image Credit: NASA and The Hubble Heritage Team (STScI/AURA)
Acknowledgment: George Herbig and Theodore Simon (Institute for Astronomy, University of Hawaii)

CREATIVE POWER

As a being of potential energy, I realize that the source of all I need is within me. I can do and become whatever I desire.

AFFIRMATIONS

I am a receptive soul for the power of God's gifts.
I am a channel for His creative energy.
He gives me His power, His powers are mine.
My desires are for good and my creativity bring blessings.
I have powers yet to be explored.

The Image: Coiled Galaxy NGC1097

There are several hundred star clusters in NGC 3310, visible in the Heritage image as the bright blue diffuse objects that trace the galaxy's spiral arms. Each of these star clusters represents the formation of up to about a million stars, a process that takes less than 100,000 years. In addition, hundreds of individual young, luminous stars can be seen throughout the galaxy. Located in the direction of the constellation Ursa Major, NGC 3310 has a distance of about 59 million light-years.

Photo and description courtesy of Hubblesite.org
Image Credit: NASA and The Hubble Heritage Team (STScI/AURA) Acknowledgment: G.R. Meurer and T.M. Heckman (JHU), C. Leitherer, J. Harris and D. Calzetti (STScI), and M. Sirianni (JHU)